D1314007

Vampire Life

by Rich Rainey

Consultant: Elizabeth Miller
Professor Emeritus
Memorial University of Newfoundland

CAPSTONE PRESS
a capstone imprint

Edge Books are published by Capstone Press,
151 Good Counsel Drive, P.O. Box 669, Mankato, Minnesota 56002.
www.capstonepub.com

Printed in the United States of America in North Mankato, Minnesota.
032010
005740CGF10

Books published by Capstone Press are manufactured with paper
containing at least 10 percent post-consumer waste.

Library of Congress Cataloging-in-Publication Data
Rainey, Rich.
  Vampire life / by Rich Rainey.
     p. cm.—(Edge books. vampires)
  Includes bibliographical references and index.
  Summary: "Presents the history behind vampire life, including their body parts,
hunting styles, and weaknesses"—Provided by publisher.
  ISBN 978-1-4296-4577-5 (library binding)
  1. Vampires—Juvenile literature. I. Title. II. Series.
GR830.V3R35 2011
398'.45—dc22   2010001692

Editorial Credits
Megan Peterson, editor; Veronica Correia, designer; Marcie Spence,
     media researcher; Laura Manthe, production specialist

Photo Credits
Ardea/Adrian Warren, 11
The Bridgeman Art Library International, 5; DACS, 9
Capstone Press, 25 (left)
The Granger Collection, New York, 17 (left)
Hulton Archive/Getty Images Inc., 7, 19 (vampire), 21; Silver Screen Collection, 12
iStockphoto/Jamesmcq24, 25 (right), 27 (stake); meltonmedia, 20; nicoolay, 27
     (heart); wwing, 27 (shovel)
Kharen Hill/The CW/Landov LLC, 17 (right)
Newscom/wenn, 23
Shutterstock/Chas, 10 (top left); Cindi L, 18 (coffin); Eric Isselee, 10 (top right);
     Margaret M Stewart, 13; Margot Petrowski, 16, 22; Maxim Kulko, 10
     (bottom); Robert Spriggs, cover, 18–19 (castle background); yazan masa,
     26–27 (flames)
Ullstein bild/The Granger Collection, New York, 14
Universal/The Kobal Collection, 29
Zoetrope/Columbia Tri-Star/The Kobal Collection/Nelson, Ralph Jr., 15

TABLE OF CONTENTS

Chapter 1

A MONSTROUS HISTORY

A thick gray fog rolls over a dark cemetery. Moonlight shines down on rows of crumbling gravestones. Tucked inside an old stone tomb sits a wooden coffin. A clawlike hand slowly pushes open the coffin's lid, and a man sits up. He's thin, pale, and hungry—for human blood.

The monsters known as vampires have haunted our imaginations for thousands of years. People once believed they were real creatures that sucked human blood. From novels like *Dracula* to movies like *Twilight*, vampires continue to spring to life today.

spirit—the invisible part of a person that contains thoughts and feelings

Vampires around the World

The idea of what a vampire is has changed over time. Greek *vrykolakas* sat on their victims' chests and crushed them to death. Arabic stories introduced the idea of demonlike vampires. They survived by eating human flesh. Legends from ancient Babylonia tell of the *edimmu*. This bloodsucking **spirit** could not rest. Instead, it was doomed to roam the Earth, hunting humans.

European Vampires

The belief in vampires was common in central and eastern Europe in the 1600s and 1700s. For hundreds of years, several **plagues** killed many people in Europe. The dead were often buried in mass graves.

People sometimes reopened the graves to make room for more dead bodies. Some recently buried bodies were **bloated**, as if they'd just been fed. Blood sometimes oozed from the bodies' mouths. People believed these corpses had become vampires. They blamed these "vampires" for spreading diseases.

Vampires in Fiction

By the 1800s, vampires had become popular subjects in books. In 1819, John Polidori published *The Vampyre: A Tale.* It was the first major vampire story printed in English. Bram Stoker's 1897 novel *Dracula* and the movies based on it popularized the idea of the good-looking, powerful vampire.

plague—a serious disease that spreads quickly to many people and often causes death
bloated—swollen with fluid or gas

Plague victims were often quickly buried in mass graves.

FACT:

The 1847 novel *Varney the Vampire* was published in weekly chapters called "penny-dreadfuls." Each chapter cost one penny.

Chapter 2

LIFE OF THE UNDEAD

A bat flutters its black wings as it lands on a windowsill. Its dark shape slowly changes into a vampire. With unblinking eyes, the vampire creeps toward a sleeping human. The bloodsucker's sharp fangs glisten in the moonlight. Suddenly, the vampire sinks its fangs into the victim's neck.

Count Dracula turned into a bloodthirsty bat in the novel *Dracula.* But changing shape is just one of many features that makes vampires terrifying. So grab your wooden stake and get ready to explore the life of the undead—if you dare.

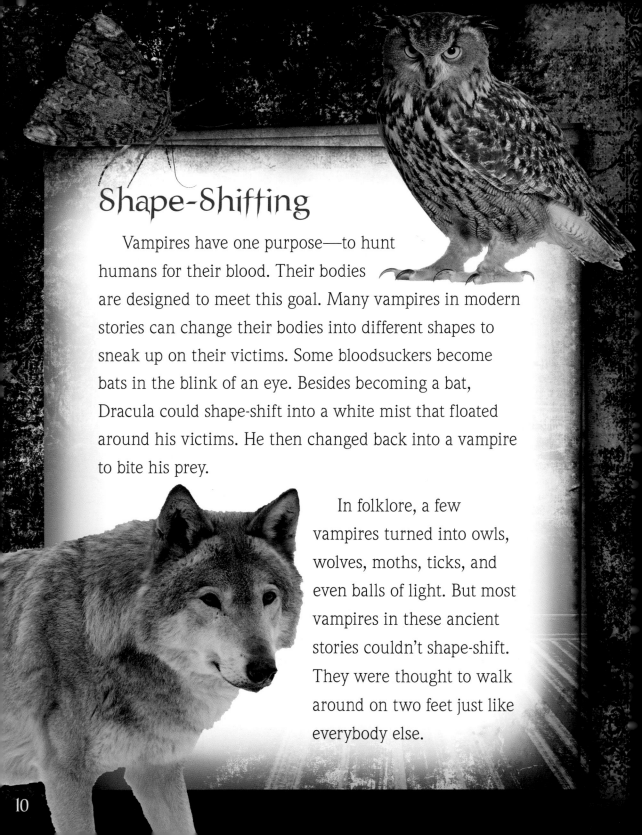

Shape-Shifting

Vampires have one purpose—to hunt humans for their blood. Their bodies are designed to meet this goal. Many vampires in modern stories can change their bodies into different shapes to sneak up on their victims. Some bloodsuckers become bats in the blink of an eye. Besides becoming a bat, Dracula could shape-shift into a white mist that floated around his victims. He then changed back into a vampire to bite his prey.

In folklore, a few vampires turned into owls, wolves, moths, ticks, and even balls of light. But most vampires in these ancient stories couldn't shape-shift. They were thought to walk around on two feet just like everybody else.

The Real Creatures of the Night

Vampires don't exist. But vampire-like creatures really do live in Central and South America. Known as vampire bats, these bloodsuckers live up to their name. They use sharp fangs to bite horses, cows, pigs, and birds. The bats then lap up the blood with their tongues.

FACT:

Bram Stoker read about vampire bats. They inspired him to give Count Dracula the power to change into a bat in his book.

Powerful Eyes

In today's legends, vampires use the "evil eye" to place humans in a dreamlike state. Sleeping vampires can still use the evil eye. Some vampires, like Count Dracula, sleep with their eyes open. Anyone brave enough to approach these vampires can be put in a trance.

Vampires with powerful eyes can also be found in folklore. One look from India's *jigarkhwar* vampire was believed to remove its victim's liver. The Russian *eretiku* could spread disease with a single glance.

Count Dracula used his powerful eyes to place victims in a trance.

Razor-Sharp Fangs

Most people are familiar with the movie vampire, who often has fangs that can slice through flesh. But vampires of folklore were thought to have regular human teeth. Others used pointed tongues to pierce their victims' skin. Novels like *Varney the Vampire* and *Dracula* gave vampires long, sharp **canine** teeth.

Thanks to the imaginations of writers and filmmakers, today's vampires often have fangs that change size. The fangs grow out from their gums like narrow, hollow tubes. When the vampires finish feeding, their fangs disappear.

FACT:

Many vampires in books and movies don't have reflections or shadows.

canine—a sharp tooth used to tear meat

Got Blood?

Vampires have a thirst for blood—human blood. In modern stories, vampires often have ghostly white skin. The pale color is a sure sign that they are running out of blood and energy. And that can only mean one thing—they need to kill another victim.

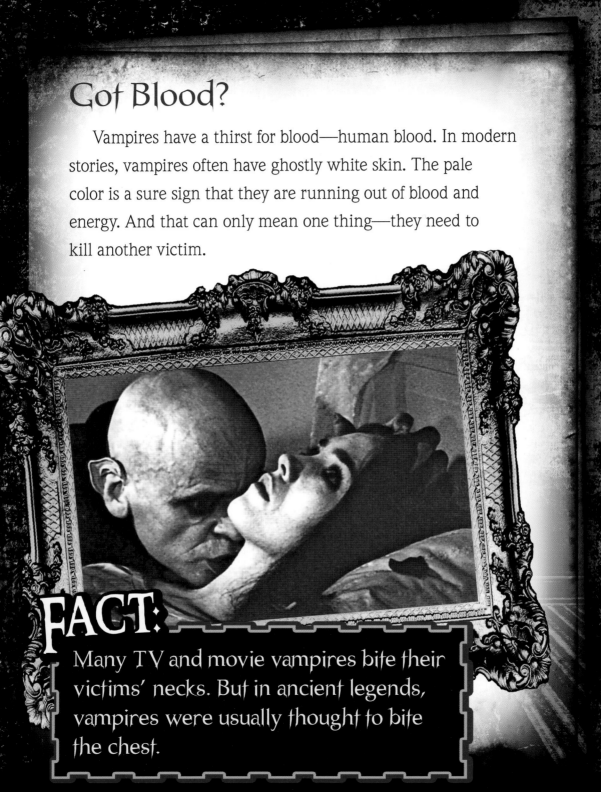

FACT:

Many TV and movie vampires bite their victims' necks. But in ancient legends, vampires were usually thought to bite the chest.

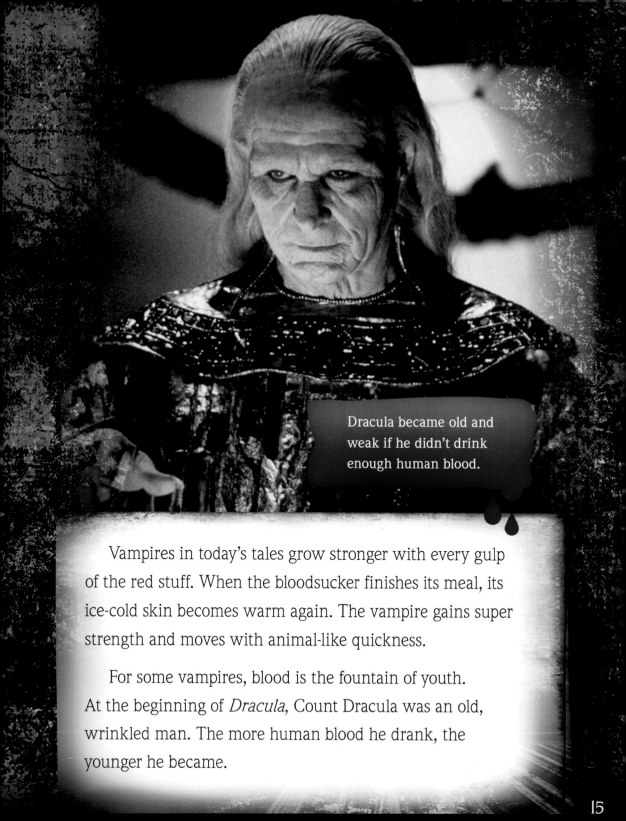

Dracula became old and weak if he didn't drink enough human blood.

Vampires in today's tales grow stronger with every gulp of the red stuff. When the bloodsucker finishes its meal, its ice-cold skin becomes warm again. The vampire gains super strength and moves with animal-like quickness.

For some vampires, blood is the fountain of youth. At the beginning of *Dracula*, Count Dracula was an old, wrinkled man. The more human blood he drank, the younger he became.

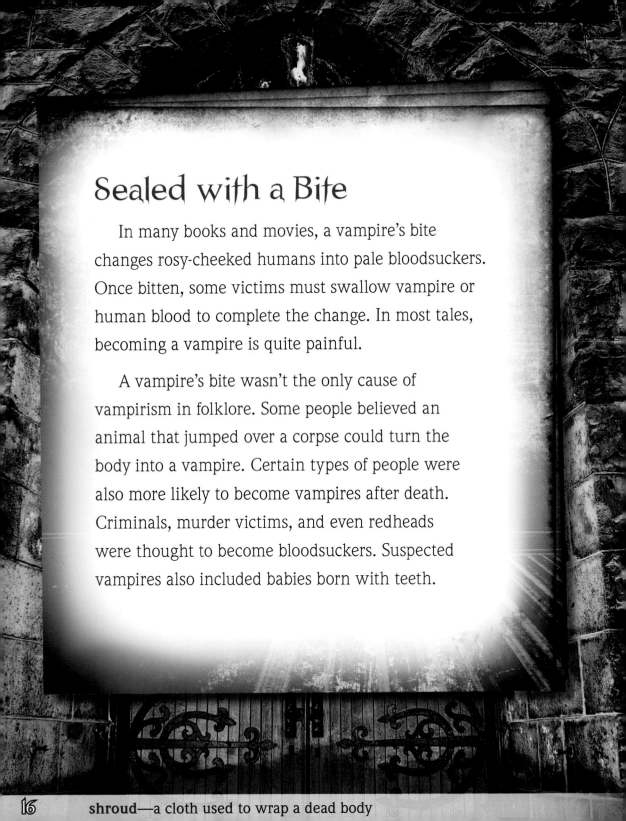

Sealed with a Bite

In many books and movies, a vampire's bite changes rosy-cheeked humans into pale bloodsuckers. Once bitten, some victims must swallow vampire or human blood to complete the change. In most tales, becoming a vampire is quite painful.

A vampire's bite wasn't the only cause of vampirism in folklore. Some people believed an animal that jumped over a corpse could turn the body into a vampire. Certain types of people were also more likely to become vampires after death. Criminals, murder victims, and even redheads were thought to become bloodsuckers. Suspected vampires also included babies born with teeth.

shroud—a cloth used to wrap a dead body

Dressed to Kill

From capes to designer jeans, the vampire look has changed over time. The vampires of European legend often wore burial **shrouds**. Later, vampires in books, movies, and TV dressed in more stylish outfits. Varney the vampire walked around town wearing a fancy suit. In the 1931 film *Dracula*, the count preferred a black suit and matching cape. Many of today's vampires dress just like regular humans.

Actor Bela Lugosi wore a cape in the 1931 movie *Dracula*.

Vampire brothers Damon (left) and Stefan (right) from *The Vampire Diaries* TV show wear the latest fashions.

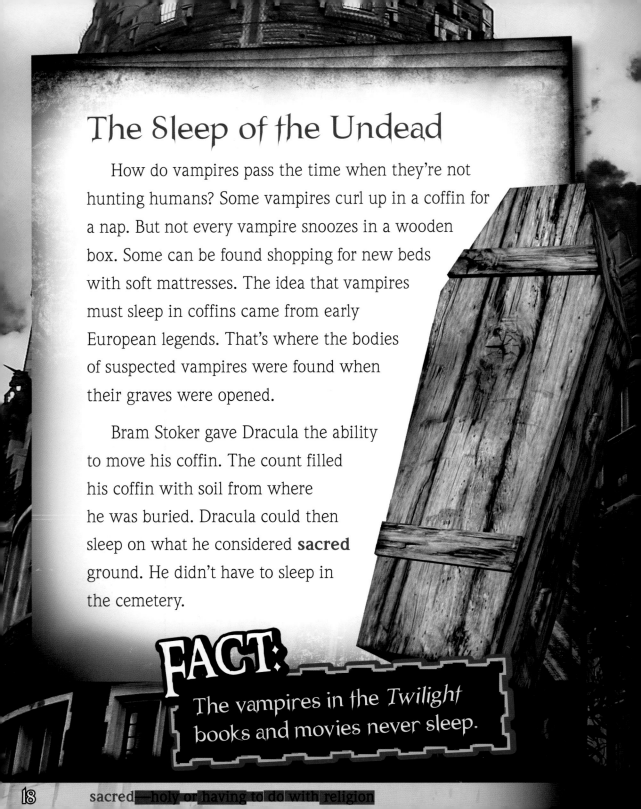

The Sleep of the Undead

How do vampires pass the time when they're not hunting humans? Some vampires curl up in a coffin for a nap. But not every vampire snoozes in a wooden box. Some can be found shopping for new beds with soft mattresses. The idea that vampires must sleep in coffins came from early European legends. That's where the bodies of suspected vampires were found when their graves were opened.

Bram Stoker gave Dracula the ability to move his coffin. The count filled his coffin with soil from where he was buried. Dracula could then sleep on what he considered **sacred** ground. He didn't have to sleep in the cemetery.

FACT:

The vampires in the *Twilight* books and movies never sleep.

sacred—holy or having to do with religion

Home Sweet Home

Whether a vampire sleeps in a coffin or a bed, every bloodsucker calls someplace home. In folklore, vampires lived wherever they were buried. In books and movies, bloodsuckers moved into more comfortable dwellings. Count Dracula lived in a large stone castle in Transylvania. Vampires in today's tales can be found anywhere, from large houses to cozy apartments.

Actor Dieter Eppler played a vampire in the 1962 movie *Curse of the Blood Ghouls.*

Not-So-Deadly Sunlight

Some vampires of folklore were thought to leave their graves only at night. But many hunted during the day. Even Count Dracula left his castle during daylight hours. His powers, however, were strongest at night. The 1922 film *Nosferatu* introduced the idea that sunlight could kill a vampire.

Today many vampire stories feature bloodsuckers that hunt during the day. Some vampires have skin that glitters instead of burning in direct sunlight. Others wear special jewelry that protects them from sunlight.

Vampire Weaknesses

With super-human strength and sharp fangs, vampires may seem unstoppable. But vampires do have a few weaknesses. In early legends, crosses and holy water were thought to keep away bad spirits, including vampires.

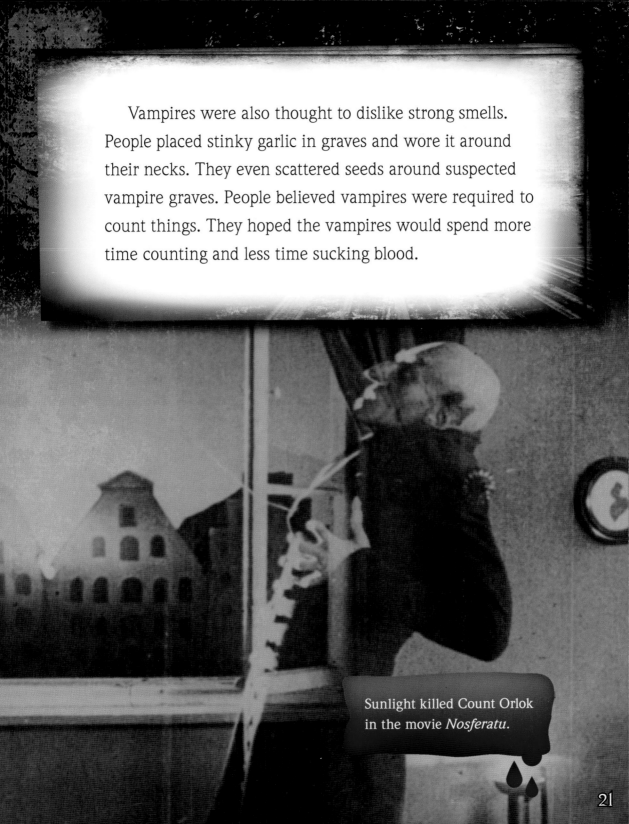

Vampires were also thought to dislike strong smells. People placed stinky garlic in graves and wore it around their necks. They even scattered seeds around suspected vampire graves. People believed vampires were required to count things. They hoped the vampires would spend more time counting and less time sucking blood.

Sunlight killed Count Orlok in the movie *Nosferatu*.

Thanks to writer Bram Stoker, vampires in modern stories must also follow some rules. These vampires usually can't enter a person's home unless invited. But once inside, they can enter again at will. Some bloodsuckers can't cross running water.

FACT:

The word "vampire" was added to the *Oxford English Dictionary* in 1734.

A Vampire's Grave

In 2006, researchers uncovered a mass grave near Venice, Italy. It contained the remains of a woman buried there in the 1500s. The woman, once thought to be a vampire, had died during a plague. A large brick had been placed between her jaws. According to legend, this would keep a suspected vampire from chewing out of the grave.

Chapter 3

THE VAMPIRE HUNTER'S GUIDE

It's a good thing vampires aren't real. But what if they were? How could we stop them? Fortunately, two vampire "experts" have provided everything we need to know about "killing" the undead.

The Real Vampire Hunter

In the early 1700s, a monk named Augustin Calmet investigated reports of vampire sightings in Europe. He wrote about them in his book *The Phantom World*. These cases often involved unexplained deaths in remote villages. The townspeople blamed the deaths on vampires.

Treatise on
VAMPIRES & REVENANTS
The Phantom World

DOM AUGUSTIN CALMET

Augustin Calmet recorded suspected vampire sightings in his book *The Phantom World.*

Calmet recorded four main ways the villagers killed suspected vampires. Any single method could supposedly stop a vampire. But to be totally safe, villagers sometimes used more than one method.

WOODEN STAKE: Villagers drove a sharp, wooden stake through the vampire's heart. Sometimes a body groaned as if still alive. Today we know the release of built-up gases caused this terrifying sound.

SPADE: Villagers chopped off the vampire's head with a spade. The head was often reburied with the body.

KNIFE: Townspeople cut out the vampire's heart. They thought this would keep the body from pumping blood.

FIRE: Some vampire bodies were burned until there was nothing left but ashes. The ashes were sometimes dumped into a nearby river.

FACT:

In Bulgaria, suspected vampires were stabbed with red-hot irons.

The Fictional Vampire Hunter

While writing *Dracula*, Bram Stoker visited the British Museum to study vampire legends. Emily Gerard's 1885 article "Transylvanian Superstitions" provided him with a great deal of vampire information. Stoker used his research to create the character of Professor Van Helsing, a fictional vampire expert in his book. Van Helsing hunted Count Dracula, the most famous vampire of all time.

Like Calmet, Van Helsing's killing methods included staking the vampire's heart and removing its head. The professor also had a few other vampire remedies up his sleeve:

Press a church wafer into the vampire's forehead. The wafer will burn its skin like acid.

Place a branch of wild roses on top of the vampire's coffin. This plant will keep the vampire inside its coffin.

Shoot the vampire with a sacred bullet.

Cut off the vampire's head, and stuff its mouth full of garlic.

Seal the body and head inside the coffin with lead.

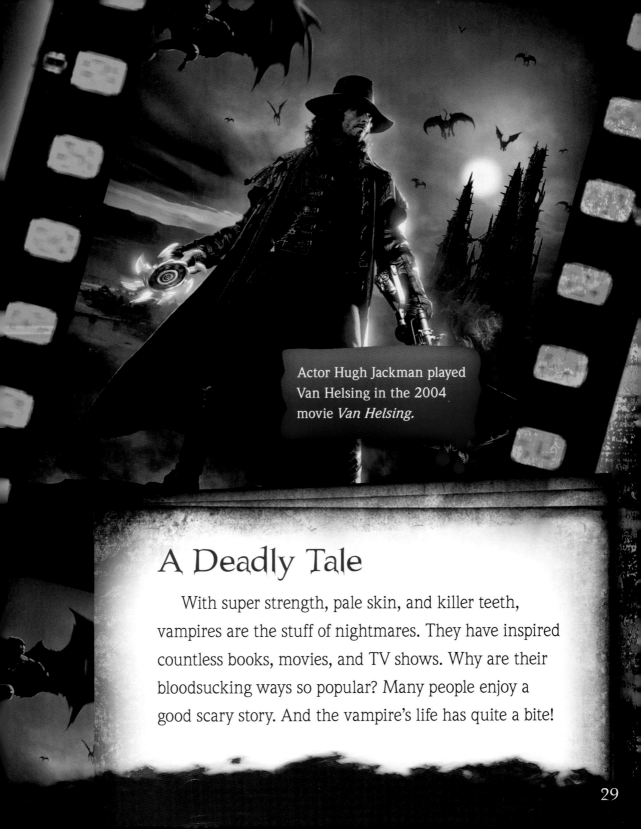

Actor Hugh Jackman played Van Helsing in the 2004 movie *Van Helsing*.

A Deadly Tale

With super strength, pale skin, and killer teeth, vampires are the stuff of nightmares. They have inspired countless books, movies, and TV shows. Why are their bloodsucking ways so popular? Many people enjoy a good scary story. And the vampire's life has quite a bite!

GLOSSARY

bloat (BLOHT)—a condition in which a dead body fills with gas or liquid as the tissues break down

canine (KAY-nine)—a sharp tooth used to tear meat

corpse (KORPS)—a dead body

folklore (FOHK-lor)—the stories, customs, and beliefs of people that are passed down to their children

plague (PLAYG)—a serious disease that spreads quickly to many people and often causes death

sacred (SAY-krid)—holy or having to do with religion

shroud (SHROUD)—a cloth used to wrap a dead body

spade (SPAYD)—a tool with a flat blade and a long handle; spades are used for digging

spirit (SPIHR-it)—the invisible part of a person that contains thoughts and feelings; some people believe the spirit leaves the body after death

trance (TRANSS)—a state in which a person is awake but not really aware of what is happening around them

READ MORE

Barnhill, Kelly Regan. *Blood-Sucking, Man-Eating Monsters.* Horrible Things. Mankato, Minn.: Capstone Press, 2009.

Gee, Joshua. *Encyclopedia Horrifica: The Terrifying Truth! About Vampires, Ghosts, Monsters, and More.* New York: Scholastic Inc., 2007.

Marx, Mandy R. *Great Vampire Legends.* Vampires. Mankato, Minn.: Capstone Press, 2011.

Oxlade, Chris. *The Mystery of Vampires and Werewolves.* Can Science Solve? Chicago: Heinemann Library, 2008.

INTERNET SITES

FactHound offers a safe, fun way to find Internet sites related to this book. All of the sites on FactHound have been researched by our staff.

Here's all you do:

Visit *www.facthound.com*

FactHound will fetch the best sites for you!

INDEX

24081 7871